# Hammy Hammerhead's
## (almost) BIG
# ADVENTURE!

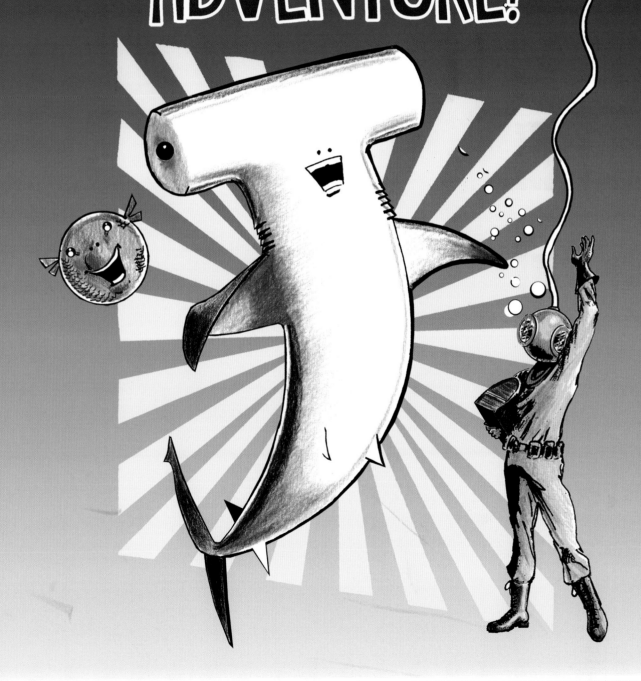

For my parents, Tom & Ann, for making me possible,
and for still believing in me.

Plus, a special thanks to everyone
who helped me fine-tune this-here bad boy!
(Especially my most-specialist junior proof-readers:
Emma, Luke, Jack, Finley, Ben & Gracie!)

And, as always,
that Sweetest Little Thing, Ever,
Gwen

# Hammy Hammerhead's (almost) Big Adventure!

## Story and Pictures by Mike Crowder

# Chapter One: SharkLand™

Now, friends, long before you were born, *high* up in the mountains of Florida, was a place named "SharkLand™,"
or, as we liked to call it:

"SharkLand™."

(I know, there aren't any
    mountains in Florida,
    but... you see...
    it's *only* a storybook.)

SharkLand™
was the biggest aquarium in the
whole United States! Maybe in
the whole world!

Now, what is
the biggest
thing you can
think of...?

It was *bigger*!

(Unless you can think
    of, like, a state, or
    maybe a planet.)

**...Land™**

Back then, *most* places had stuff like sea lions, orcas, and dolphins.

*Not* SharkLand™! *It* was *all* sharks, *all* the time!

## Chapter Two:
## In Which Hammy Cleans His Room

Mama Hammerhead came downstairs to find Hammy eating breakfast. "Morning, Hammy! Have you cleaned your room, yet?"

CHUM-O'S

sum orem

Merol Muspi

Prize Inside!!

"No Ma'am."

"I'll jump right on it, once I've polished off this chummy bowl of Yum-O's™!" He snorted. "I mean, yummy bowl of Chum-O's™!"

Mama replied, "Hampton J. Hammerhead!"

"And don't you make me come up there...!" Mama called.

Hammy slumped on his bottom bunk.
He had hoped faeries or elves might clean his room
whilst he was eating; clearly 'twas not to be...
"Dang it...!" he thought, "Just like last time!"

"It's not fair!"

(Now, friends, it really wasn't. Because *everyone* knows magical
creatures help *only* penniless shoemakers with *lots* of kids.)

(And who wants to clean some kid's bedroom?)

9

It took Hammy only three minutes and eight seconds 'til he was out the front door!

(I *know*, right? Cleaning your room *can* be hard, just not this time!)

"Great Chum-O's, Mama, but I have to motor if I want to play pufferball!"

"Be back before dark, Little Pup!"

"Aww, Ma!"

(Young sharks are called 'pups'! ...Just like young seals!)

"Morning, Mr. Porter!"
Hammy waved to the old-timey diver guy you
see at the bottom of every fish tank.

But, few sharks speak "People" and even
*fewer* people speak "Shark." So, what the
diver heard was, "Glug, glug, glug,"
and he just waved back to Hammy.

(Now friends, that's what *I* would have done.)

(I mean, Hammy *was* a shark.)

(*A shark*!)

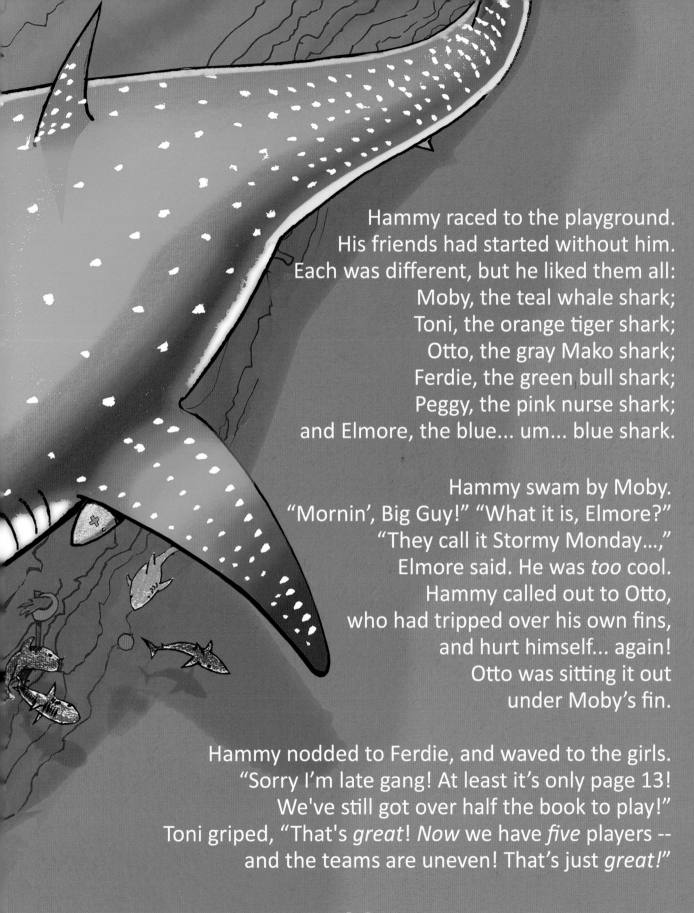

Hammy raced to the playground.
His friends had started without him.
Each was different, but he liked them all:
Moby, the teal whale shark;
Toni, the orange tiger shark;
Otto, the gray Mako shark;
Ferdie, the green bull shark;
Peggy, the pink nurse shark;
and Elmore, the blue... um... blue shark.

Hammy swam by Moby.
"Mornin', Big Guy!" "What it is, Elmore?"
"They call it Stormy Monday...,"
Elmore said. He was *too* cool.
Hammy called out to Otto,
who had tripped over his own fins,
and hurt himself... again!
Otto was sitting it out
under Moby's fin.

Hammy nodded to Ferdie, and waved to the girls.
"Sorry I'm late gang! At least it's only page 13!
We've still got over half the book to play!"
Toni griped, "That's *great*! *Now* we have *five* players --
and the teams are uneven! That's just *great!*"

"We can fit you you in!" laughed Peggy.

Now friends, pufferball is just like basketball, only with a Pufferfish as a ball. But Pufferfish *float*, so they have to be thrown from *under* the basket...

Pufferball is hard!

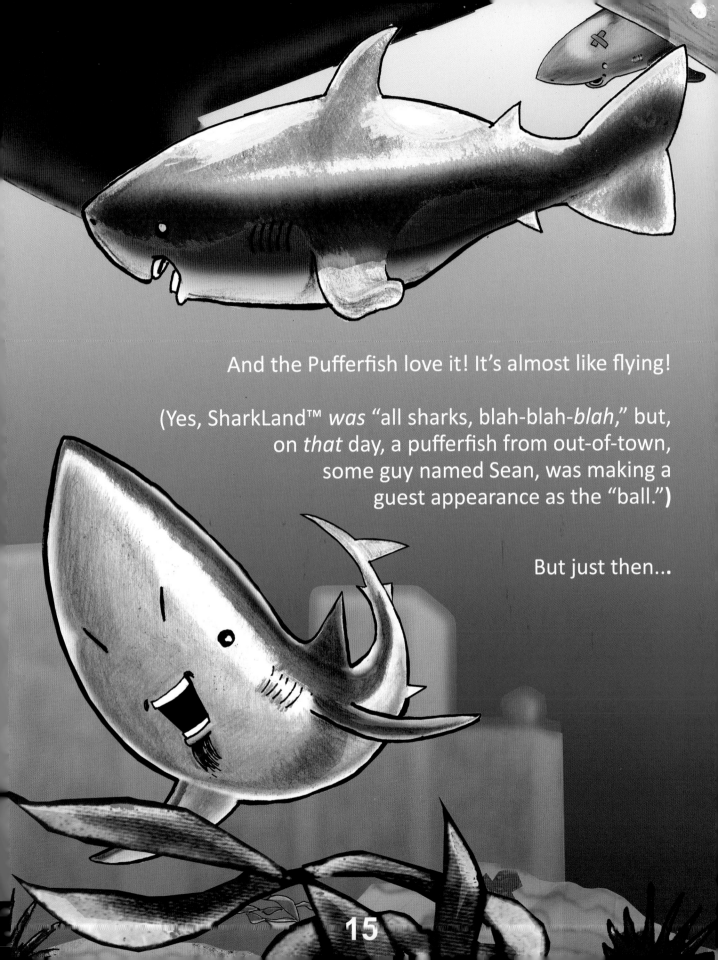

And the Pufferfish love it! It's almost like flying!

(Yes, SharkLand™ *was* "all sharks, blah-blah-*blah*," but, on *that* day, a pufferfish from out-of-town, some guy named Sean, was making a guest appearance as the "ball.")

But just then...

Holy Mackere[

It was the school bully, Spike!
He charged Toni, and stole Sean away!

As Toni began to cry, Spike began
to laugh just like a *Clownfish*!

*If* that Clownfish were
*really* big,
*really* mean,
and *really* scary!

18

"Dang it, Spike! What is your damage?" shouted Hammy. "Give Sean back to Toni, and try picking on someone your own size!"

Spike laughed. "What're you going to do about it, *shrimp*?"

"I'm not a shrimp! I'm 'fun-sized!'" Hammy replied.

Hammy looked to his friends for help. Moby could have squashed Spike by sitting on him, but he was too slow. Ferdie was a "Fraidy Catfish," Otto, too clumsy.

Elmore was just too cool.

Hammy looked down.
"Look, man, it's already page 21."
"We've got just 11 pages left!"
"If I can beat you at free throws, will you
just get out of our gills, and go away?"
"Sure, shrimpy!" sneered Spike.
"The winner is the first to
float three baskets!"

Now, it was all up to "fun-sized" Hammy against the big bully. Spike was the best pufferball player at the playground, but, Hammy wasn't sweating it, because he had been practicing free throws in the driveway!

*83 whole* minutes went by, yet
*still* they were tied with only two baskets each!

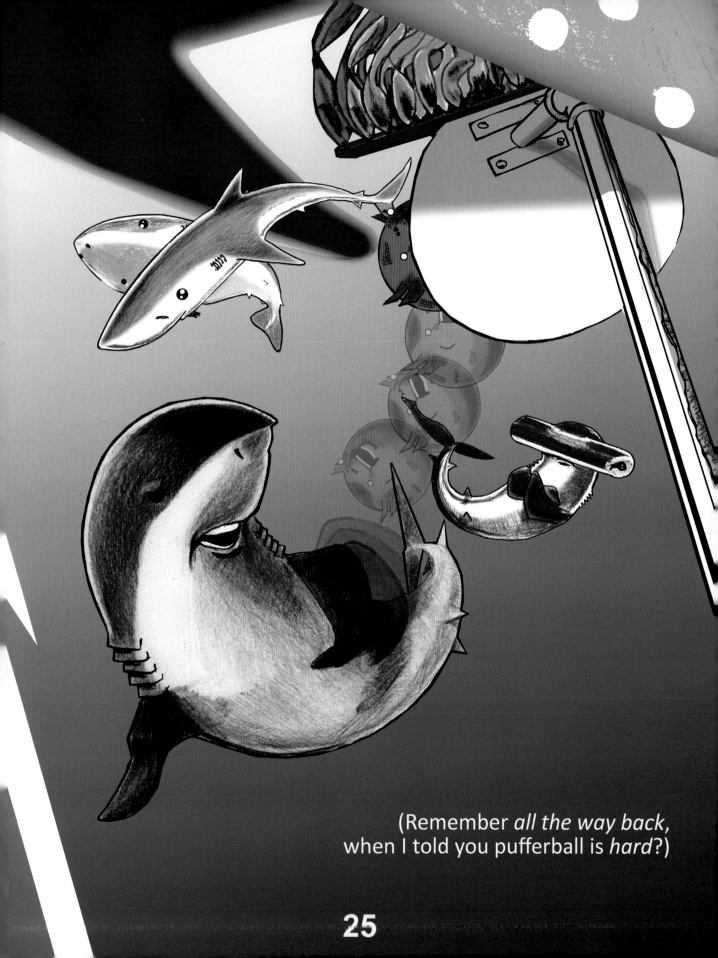

(Remember *all the way back*,
when I told you pufferball is *hard*?)

At last, Hammy got his *third* basket! Behind his head! Just like that famous basketball player!

(You know... *that guy*! He plays for that team? They win a lot?)

26

Spike swam away, because he knew
he'd been beaten.
The other pups laughed at him.

(Except Elmore. *You* know why.)

Hammy shook his head.
His pals were just
being bullies like Spike!

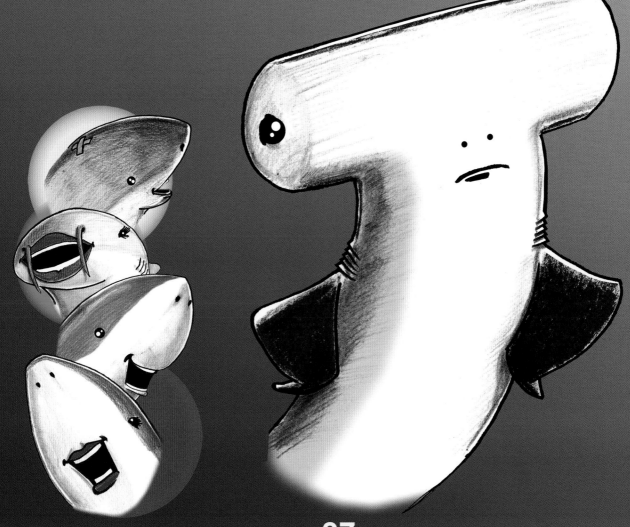

"Y'all are just being bullies like Spike!" he said.

"Did y'all learn *nothing* today?"

28

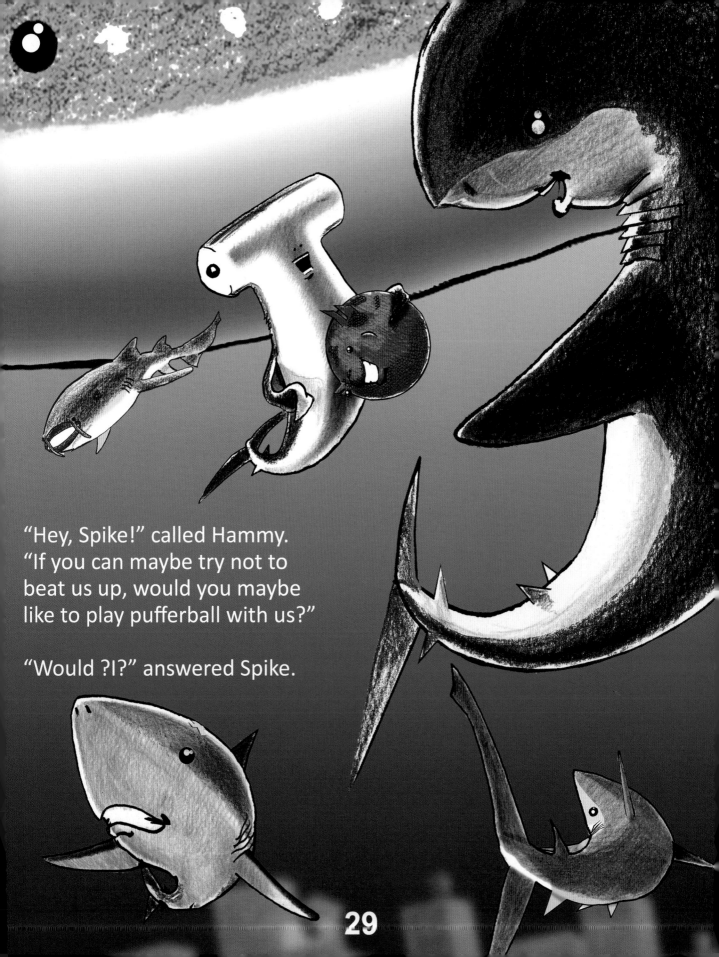

"Hey, Spike!" called Hammy.
"If you can maybe try not to
beat us up, would you maybe
like to play pufferball with us?"

"Would ?I?" answered Spike.

"Well, since we're the two best players,
Spike and I will face the rest of y'all."
said Hammy.

"Toni's team can be the 'shirts,'
and we'll be the 'skins,'"
he chuckled. "*Shark*skins...!"

(Moby even moved far away,
just so you can see him!)

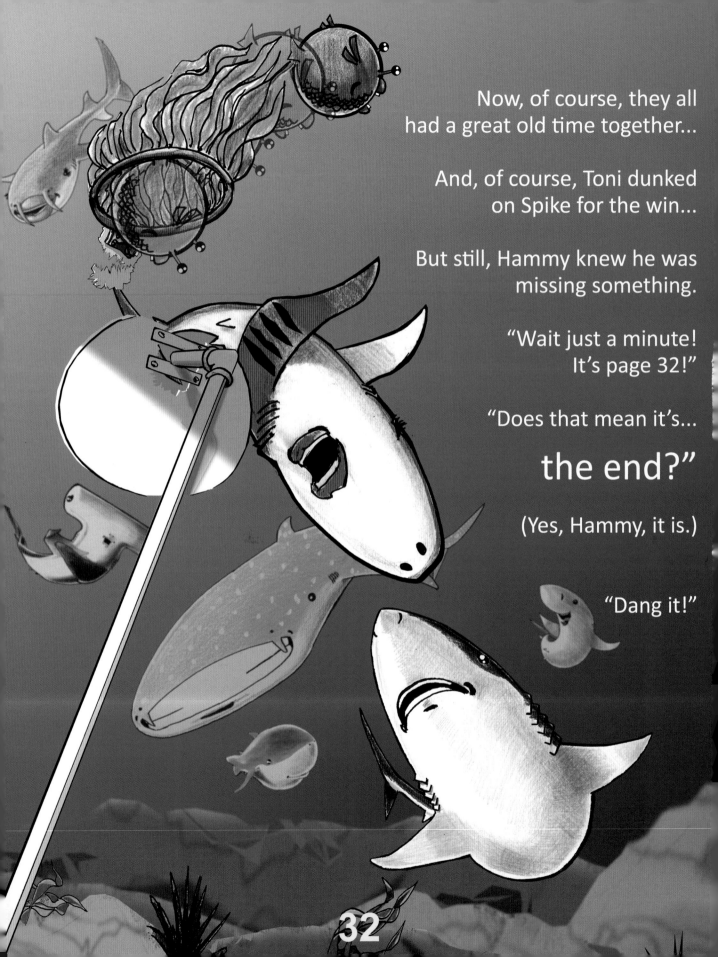

Now, of course, they all had a great old time together...

And, of course, Toni dunked on Spike for the win...

But still, Hammy knew he was missing something.

"Wait just a minute! It's page 32!"

"Does that mean it's...

the end?"

(Yes, Hammy, it is.)

"Dang it!"